I can do it!

Bobbie Kalman

Crabtree Publishing Company
www.crabtreebooks.com

Created by Bobbie Kalman

Author and Editor-in-Chief
Bobbie Kalman

Educational consultants
Reagan Miller
Elaine Hurst
Joan King

Editors
Reagan Miller
Joan King
Kathy Middleton

Proofreader
Crystal Sikkens

Design
Bobbie Kalman
Katherine Berti

Production coordinator
Katherine Berti

Prepress technician
Katherine Berti

Photographs
Katherine Berti: p. 6 (shapes)
iStockphoto: cover (girl), p. 7
All other photographs by Shutterstock

Library and Archives Canada Cataloguing in Publication

Kalman, Bobbie, 1947-
I can do it! / Bobbie Kalman.

(My world)
ISBN 978-0-7787-9423-3 (bound).--ISBN 978-0-7787-9467-7 (pbk.)

1. Ability--Juvenile literature. 2. Self-actualization (Psychology)--Juvenile literature. I. Title. II. Series: My world (St. Catharines, Ont.)

BF637.S4K33 2010 j158.1 C2009-906059-0

Library of Congress Cataloging-in-Publication Data

Kalman, Bobbie.
I can do it! / Bobbie Kalman.
p. cm. -- (My world)
ISBN 978-0-7787-9467-7 (pbk. : alk. paper) -- ISBN 978-0-7787-9423-3 (reinforced library binding : alk. paper)
1. Early childhood education--Activity programs--Juvenile literature. 2. Reading (Early childhood)--Juvenile literature. 3. Handicraft--Juvenile literature. I. Title. II. Series.

LB1139.35.A37K355 2010
372.21--dc22

2009040960

Crabtree Publishing Company

Printed in Canada/092023/CPC20230912

www.crabtreebooks.com 1-800-387-7650

 In Canada: We acknowledge the financial support of the Government of Canada through the Canada Book Fund for our publishing activities.

Published in Canada
Crabtree Publishing
616 Welland Ave.
St. Catharines, Ontario
L2M 5V6

Published in the United States
Crabtree Publishing
347 Fifth Ave
Suite 1402-145
New York, NY 10016

Published in the United Kingdom
Crabtree Publishing
Maritime House
Basin Road North, Hove
BN41 1WR

Published in Australia
Crabtree Publishing
Unit 3-5
Currumbin Court
Capalaba QLD 4157

Words to know

baseball

dolphin

drums

laptop computer

tiger cub

I can read.
I read with my friend.
We like to read stories.

I can write.
I can write about anything.
I like to write stories.

I can do math.
I can count to ten.
I can draw shapes.

I can use a **laptop computer**.
I can learn new things.
I can send emails.

I can swim under water.
I can hold my breath.
I like to swim in a pool.

I can play **baseball**.
I can hit the ball.

I can sing.
I know a lot of songs.
I like to sing happy songs.

I can play the **drums**.
I can keep the beat.
I like to play loud music.

I can help take care of others.
I can babysit my little sister.

I can learn about animals.
I can find out how to help them.
I am feeding a **tiger cub**.

Activity

Name five things that you can do.

Are there some things that you can do very well?

What are they?

What would you like to do that you have never done before? Would you like to swim with a **dolphin**?

Notes for adults

Goal-setting

I can do it! What are the things that children can do? As an extension activity to accompany this book, children can work on building goal-setting skills. Setting goals is an important skill that will help children throughout their lives.

Action plans

Ask the children to make a list of all the things they do well. Next, ask them to choose skills that they want to learn or improve, such as reading, swimming, or playing a certain sport or musical instrument. Ask them to choose one really big challenge in their lives that they want to overcome. Brainstorm ways that they could accomplish their goals. Help them write an action plan or have them draw pictures to accompany their plans. Ask them to post their action plans in their bedrooms or in other places where they can see them often. Have them review their plans throughout the year to gauge their progress.

Dream boards

Have the children make three "I can do it!" dream boards:

1. Things I can do (for confidence)
2. Things I am learning to do (for motivation)
3. Things I want to do in the future (for positive imaging)

Children can draw pictures or cut them out of magazines to make each dream board. Each board will be a visual collage that will help the children gain confidence and create positive life goals.